Concord Village

A Guided Walk Through the Past

Ron McAdow

PHP

Personal History Press
Lincoln, Massachusetts

Monument Square circa 1830

Courtesy Concord Free Public Library Corporation

Contents

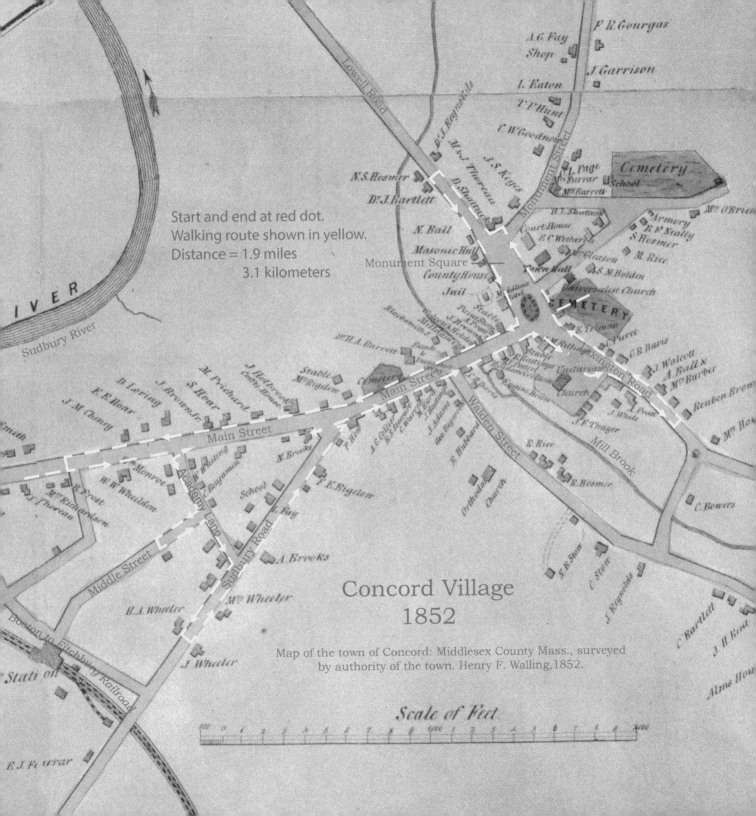

Start and end at red dot.
Walking route shown in yellow.
Distance = 1.9 miles
    3.1 kilometers

Concord Village
1852

Map of the town of Concord: Middlesex County Mass., surveyed
by authority of the town. Henry F. Walling, 1852.

Scale of Feet

RIVER

Sudbury River

Lowell Road

Monument Street

Monument Square

Main Street

Walden Street

Academy Lane

Sudbury Road

Middle Street

Lexington Road

Mill Brook

Boston to Fitchburg Railroad

Station

Cemetery

Cemetery

Cemetery

School

Armory

Court House

Town Hall

Masonic Hall

CountyHouse

Jail

Bank

Universalist Church

Orthodox Church

F. R. Gourgas
A. G. Fay Shop
J. Garrison
I. Eaton
T. F. Hunt
C. W. Goodnow
Dr J. Reynolds
Mrs J. Thoreau
J. S. Keyes
N. S. Hosmer
D. Shattuck
Dr J. Bartlett
I. Page
Mrs Farrar
T. McBarrett
H. J. Shattuck
Mrs O'Brien
N. Ball
R. F. Nealty
S. Hosmer
M. Clason
M. Rice
J. S. M. Holden
E. B. Davis
Dr H. A. Barrett
E. Tolman
J. Walcott
A. Ball
Mrs Barber
E. B. Davis
M. Pritchard
M. Bigelow
Stable
J. Whitc
J. Prad
Reuben Brown
J. F. Trager
Mrs Hes
D. Loring
E. R. Hoar
J. Brennan
S. Hoar
J. Hosmer
Stable
J. M. Cheney
Smith
E. Rice
R. Hosmer
R. Frost
Mrs Richardson
W. W. Wheildon
Monroe
Whiting
Benjamin
School
N. Brooks
P. Bull
T. F. Bigelow
I. Fay
C. Bowers
A. Brooks
N. B. Stow
C. Stow
J. Reynolds
H. A. Wheeler
Mrs Wheeler
J. Wheeler
C. Bartlett
J. H. Bent
Mrs Thoreau
E. J. Farrar
Alms House

Welcome to Concord's Central Village!

The town of Concord includes several "villages"—concentrations of commercial and residential development that do not have separate governance and lack precise boundaries. Many Massachusetts towns refer to such neighborhoods as villages. Usually, the site of original colonial settlement is thought of as the center, and that is the case in Concord. Concord was settled by English colonists in 1635; this walk begins and ends near the location of the first meetinghouse.

Concord was Massachusetts's first inland colonial town. In the 1620s, English Puritans began settling at Cape Ann. From 1630 to 1640, a flood of these religious dissenters sailed for New England, and tidewater towns such as Boston, Cambridge, and Watertown soon ran out of suitable farmland. Winters here were longer than those in old England; farmers found they needed plenty of hay to see their oxen through to spring. Once the salt marsh acres were spoken for, attention shifted to river meadows. The earliest inland towns, Concord, Dedham, and Sudbury, had large expanses of freshwater marsh. Musketaquid, the Algonquian name for this area, referred to the abundant grass.

The earliest history of Concord, published in 1835, said, "The uniform custom of the early settlers of the Massachusetts colony was first to obtain liberty of the government to commence a new settlement, and afterwards to acquire a full title to the soil by purchase of the Indians."[1] In 1637, two years after colonists began living at the place that had been re-named Concord, native leaders met with the newcomers, accepted gifts or payments, and signed a document that the English considered title to thirty-six square miles of land. We don't how this transaction was perceived by all parties, but, for whatever combination of reasons, this area's natives accepted the expansion of colonial settlement.[2]

In subsequent decades, officially recognized communities of "praying Indians" were established at nearby towns. The largest and longest lasting was Natick. Natives continued to market their wares in Concord through the days of the Transcendentalists, two centuries after English settlement.

When the Massachusetts General Court authorized creation of a new town at Musketaquid, it empowered settlers to impress ox carts to help them move here. The immigrants brought their contemporary technology such as metal tools for farming and woodworking and millstones for converting grain to flour. As soon as a stream could be dammed to power a mill, the energy of falling water was put to grinding grain and turning logs into boards.

The colonists arrived with well-formed cultural predilections, including a social hierarchy based on birth, wealth, and education, strict Protestant religious doctrines, and, as was revealed, a yen for self-government, which meant government by the white males who had a decent amount of property and belonged to the church. For many years there was only one official church in each Massachusetts town.

This self-guided walk, just under two miles in length, takes us along some of Concord's earliest streets. It can be done in segments suited to your stamina. The sidewalks are level; the only climb is at the Hill Burying Ground.

These pages have information on many of the structures you will pass. Most of them are houses, and most of those are in active use as dwellings. Please respect the privacy of the current residents. Although they are proud of the historic significance of their houses, do remember that while for us this village can be an outdoor museum, for the residents it is their neighborhood and home.

A large bell is mounted in the lawn in front of the First Parish Church—a bell that rang on auspicious occasions in local and American history. Our walk begins at the bell. Its location is indicated by a red dot on the map on the first page.

Lexington Road

First Parish in Concord

20 Lexington Road

The institution this building represents has been in continuous existence since 1636. The building before you is the parish's fourth meetinghouse. The first, much smaller, is thought to have stood behind you, at or near the stone house. The second meetinghouse, built in 1673, was on this side of the road. It was replaced in 1712 by a third building which was at this location but faced Monument Square. Originally a rather plain structure, it was enlarged in 1792 and a spire was added. In 1841 that building was updated to the Greek Revival style and rotated to face Lexington Road. That third meetinghouse was destroyed by fire in 1900, damaging the old bell. The church we see today was rebuilt from the plans of its predecessor.

It would be difficult to overstate the importance of the church in the history of the town. It was the dominant governing force, and its minister was the most important citizen. Town politics were also church politics. The first minister was Rev. Peter Bulkeley, who was succeeded by his son Edward.

Here met the first Provincial Congress, in 1774, and again in 1775 to discuss preparations for the war than began, nearby, shortly thereafter.

Church Green

Look to your left, past the big sycamore tree, at the two small structures. They are remnants of Concord's first center of commerce and craft.

Hosmer/Thayer House, Church Green

The building on the right, the Hosmer/Thayer House, was built around 1800. Carpenter and builder Nathan Hosmer lived here in the early 1800s. In 1846, wheelwright Isaac Thayer bought the place for his home, and worked in a shop nearby.

Munroe/White Cottage, Church Green

On the left stands the William Munroe/Joseph White Cottage, one of the oldest buildings in Concord—it might date back to the 1650s. Between 1811 and 1820 it was occupied by William Munroe, Sr. and his family. The William Munroes, senior and junior, will be mentioned frequently on our walk. Both were important citizens of Concord.

The elder Munroe began as a cabinetmaker, producing mahogany cases for the clocks his brothers made on the Milldam, and furniture. The War of 1812 altered economic conditions and created a need for goods that had previously been imported from England. Munroe decided to make pencils. He and his wife Martha first processed the graphite here—their method was a trade secret. Their business succeeded, and they moved to bigger quarters.

A wood-cutter named Joseph White owned the cottage from 1842 to 1875. It was later purchased by the parish and was long used as the residence of the church sexton.

Bundle of pencils, William Munroe
Concord, Massachusetts about 1840. Concord Museum Collection, Gift of Mr. Charles P. Munroe and Mr. William M. Munroe; 2007.261.22.

Tall Clock
Daniel Munroe and
William Munroe
Concord, Massachusetts, about 1800. Concord Museum Collection, Anonymous Gift and Gift of the Cummings Davis Society; 1995.17.

To Journeymen Cabinet Makers.
WANTED, immediately, TWO JOURNEYMAN CABINET-MAKERS, to assist in manufacturing BLACK LEADPENCILS—one year's constant employ can be given to good, industrious workmen, by application to the Subscriber, on the Mill-dam, Concord, who has for sale BLACK LEAD PENCILS, by the single one, by the dozen, groce, and by the hundred groce, and warranted good, and cheaper than can be imported.
WILLIAM MUNROE.
Concord, Jan. 30.

Advertisement in the *Middlesex Gazette*
Saturday, February 6, 1819
Courtesy Concord Free Public Library

Head east on Lexington Road toward the yellow house.

Jonathan Prescott House

48 Lexington Road

Jonathan Prescott bought this house from leather worker Isaac Meriam in 1754. It had been built in the 1720s. Its first occupant was a tailor named Joseph Wesson.

Notice, as you walk east on Lexington Road, a ridge that runs east-west behind the houses across the road. Concord's first English colonists dug their initial habitations into the south-facing slope of the hill, sheltered from north wind and open to the sun. Continue east, and cross at the crosswalk .

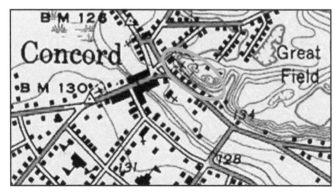

The south-facing ridge marked by the ellipse was the site of the first colonial settlement.

Concord Quadrangle, USGS Topographical Map, 1943

Reuben Brown House

77 Lexington Road

The Reuben Brown House is one of Concord's most notable historic houses. Peter Bulkeley, grandson of Concord's first pastor, built the first house here about 1667. In 1725, Peter's grandson John sold the property to a trader named Francis Fletcher, who built this house. Its steeply pitched roof and the symmetry of its façade place it in the transition between First Period and Georgian architecture (see page 40).

This neighborhood became a center of leather workers. The house passed from one saddle-maker to another after 1750. It was acquired by a young craftsman from Sudbury, Reuben Brown, in 1773. He bought the house, barn, shop, and seven acres for 190 pounds, 13 shillings. Two years later, on the day of the fight at the bridge, Reuben Brown was sent on reconnaissance to Lexington to report on the progress of the British march.

Brown prospered after the war. Like other successful Concord men, he joined a group called the Social Circle that met weekly to discuss community affairs.

The Brown family continued in this house until 1854, when it was purchased by George and Julia Clark, who also bought the house next door. Mrs. Clark took boarders in both houses. The Emerson family lodged their overflow guests with Mrs. Clark, and Mr. Emerson used the front east room as a study. He had his own study in his nearby house, which is a long block down the road, but in the years of his celebrity he needed a refuge from uninvited callers. If I lived in this house, I would imagine the sound of Emerson's feet climbing the stairs, ascending to peace and solitude.

In 1887 the house was purchased by the Concord Antiquarian Society, forerunner of the Concord Museum. In 1930, when the Antiquarian Society moved to new fireproof quarters down the road, Frederick Child bought the old house. He ran a restaurant and inn called "The Old Mill Dam" here until 1946. The house has been a single-family residence since 1955.

Antique postcard of Reuben Brown House
Courtesy Concord Free Public Library Corporation

Jonathan Fiske House

69 Lexington Road

The early history of this house is linked to the Reuben Brown house; both were part of the Bulkeley estate, both were associated with the production of leather goods, and for a long time they had common ownership. Jonathan Fiske lived here in 1724, so we know the house is at least that old. Fiske made saddles. The property passed through several hands before Reuben Brown bought it in 1773. The fact that the house is not centered around the door, but extends to the east, is probably related to its use for manufacturing—it was Reuben Brown's shop. As the British were leaving town on the day of the fight, they looted the shop and appropriated Brown's chaise to carry some of their wounded. They left the shop ablaze, but the fire was extinguished and the vehicle was later recovered.

Julia Clark and her husband lived here and boarded guests. They also sold gravel from the ridge behind the house, resulting in a gap that made space for two more houses.[3]

John Adams House

57 Lexington Road

The John Adams House has nothing to do with the presidents of that name, who were from Quincy. This John Adams was a storekeeper. The history of the property begins long before Adams built this house. In 1730 there was a tavern here. Town government's legislative branch was, as it remains, a meeting of all the voters. The executive branch was, and is, a small group called the Selectmen ("men" is now usually replaced by "board"). The Selectmen met here in Thomas Munroe's tavern until the Wright Tavern was built in 1747. The Selectmen were not paid for their service, but the town did pick up the cost of their food and drink.

By 1751 there were two other small buildings here, where craftspeople made items such as clocks, barrels, and sleigh bells. Captain John Adams came to Concord to keep a store across the street, on the church green. In 1817, having acquired this lot, he demolished the three buildings and built this house in the Federal style. This and several other of Concord's Federal Period houses have distinctive brick ends that incorporate chimneys.

Adams was a big, affable man who enjoyed playing checkers and earned a reputation for sloth. He had an energetic wife and three lively daughters, who apparently did a good job with the store. Adams belonged to the Social Circle until 1831, when the family moved to Lowell.

A well-known musician named Thomas Whitney Surrette, whose first job had been as organist at the nearby church, lived here early in the 20th century. He and his wife Ada Elizabeth Miles opened the Concord Summer School of Music in 1915, which ran for twenty-three years. The family continued at this address until Thomas Surrette died in 1941.

Thomas Dane House

47 Lexington Road

Built around 1657, this is one of Concord's oldest houses. The steep pitch of the roof is characteristic of "First Period" colonial architecture.

Thomas Dane was a carpenter. He accompanied Rev. Peter Bulkeley from

England with the understanding that he would build a house and a mill for the minister. Dane bought this land from Bulkeley and, presumably built his own house, which remained in the Dane family until 1724 when an innkeeper named Jonathan Ball purchased the place. Around 1750 his son, John Ball, a silversmith, built the next house we'll come to, although he and his family lived here. Several pieces of Ball's silver work are owned by the Concord Museum.

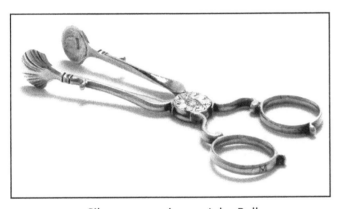

Silver sugar scissors, John Ball
Concord, Massachusetts, about 1765. Concord Museum Collection, Gift of the Cummings Davis Society; 1993.2.

Dr. Joseph Hunt owned this house by 1793. In 1953, Concord historian Ruth Robinson Wheeler published a column in the Concord Journal about local physicians that included this paragraph:

> Joseph Hunt, born in Concord in 1749, youngest son of Deacon Simon Hunt, graduated from Harvard in 1770 and studied under Dr. Cuming and went to practice in Dracut but his intellectual curiosity had been aroused and he was caught robbing a grave in Dracut for the

purpose of dissection. He was compelled publicly to re-inter the body, go down on bended knee and ask pardon of the relatives and he left Dracut in disgrace. Back in Concord, he did not try to practice at first but taught the town school for two years and married Lucy Whiting, daughter of Thomas Whiting, fourth minister of the church. He was elected to the Social Circle and was an honored and respected citizen. As ill health made the practice of medicine hard, he opened an apothecary shop in his front room (now the Tweed Shop). His nephew, William Whiting, came to live with him and rode to Boston at the age of thirteen to bring back medicines in his saddlebag. The Whitings later had a successful carriage manufacturing business on Main Street and Academy Lane.[4]

John Ball House

37 Lexington Road

Most of this house was built about 1752, but the recessed wing was added around 1815. The young silversmith John Ball had it built. Sally Lee Munroe and her husband Nathaniel Munroe, a clockmaker, lived here in the early 19th century. It was subsequently owned by

Elizabeth Roberts. *Women Sewing for Belgian Refugees*,
1914, oil on canvas board, 10.75 x 13.5 inches.
Permanent Collection Concord Art

29 Lexington Road

storekeeper Charles Davis, grocer Joel Walcott,
and his son Charles, an attorney.

In 1922 the house was purchased by a painter,
Elizabeth Wentworth Roberts, who founded
the Concord Art Association and bought the
house to be the organization's headquarters.
Roberts hired Cambridge architect Lois Lilley
Howe to adapt the old house into an art gallery
while preserving its character. (The center
chimney is a dummy, supported on steel
beams above a large gallery.) Claude Monet,
Mary Cassatt, and John Singer Sargent were
among those in attendance at the May 1923
opening.

Beaton/Davis Store

John Beaton acquired this location in 1753
for a store. It was long a venue for retail and
manufacturing. Around 1805, William Whiting

worked here as an apprentice to Henry
Sanderson, learning to make carriages. Whiting
went on to a successful career in that business
on Main Street.
Charles Davis,
when he lived next
door, had his store
and post office
here. He enlarged
the premises to
what we see today.
The building
was eventually
converted to
residential
apartments but is
now a single-family
dwelling.

Display advertisement
Yeoman Gazette
Courtesy Concord Free Public Library Corporation

Cyrus Pierce Stone House

23 Lexington Road

Concord's first meeting house was at or near this location, possibly on the hill behind. About 1730, Benjamin Barrett had a blacksmith shop here.

Cyrus Pierce, a stone mason, lived on Monument Square until Concord decided to build a town hall. Knowing that he must relocate, in 1850, Pierce bought this land and built a dwelling that advertised his skill. The ell at the back was for his mother-in-law—it was known as "Grandma's part." Cyrus and his wife Susan Ann Parks had ten children, two of whom, Frank and Arthur, had a shoe-shop on the Milldam for half a century. This unique house is one of Concord's few of the style called Gothic Revival.

Pellet-Barrett-Tolman House

5 Lexington Road

This house stands on some of the land carpenter Thomas Dane purchased from Rev. Bulkeley in 1657. Dane's daughter Mary married Thomas Pellet, sexton of the then-adjacent church. His duties included taking care of the meeting house and digging graves, and part of his compensation was use of the town's cow. Their house, willed to them in 1676, was a small building which became an ell at the rear of the big house in front of you.

In the winter, children were allowed to leave the frigid meetinghouse to warm themselves at the nearby Pellet hearth. On one such occasion, mischievous young persons put tobacco into a pot of stew simmering over the fire. The adult Pellets' suspicions were aroused by giggles from Mary Power, Hannah Stannup, and Peter Rice. The county court awarded damages to the Pellets for the ruined meal.

The original house passed through generations of Pellets before Benjamin Barrett purchased it in 1729. At that point the main house was partially constructed. Barrett completed the house, siding the place with imitation-stone stucco. Later in the century the house was owned by Abel Barrett, who kept a store on the site where St. Bernard's Church is now. Elisha Tolman, a shoemaker, bought the place from Barrett heirs in 1818. His son, a printer, probably sheltered persons fleeing enslavement before the Civil War.

In the 20th century the Old Concord Chapter of the Daughters of the American Revolution had their headquarters here. The wing at your right was constructed as their meeting place. They rented out the residence.

Tolman Shops

1 Lexington Road

Our tour of the Lexington Road houses ends with this example of the Federal style, complete with gambrel[5] roof, "lights" around the door—the small panes above and along the sides—and brick ends with their built-in chimneys. Of this place, Ruth Wheeler wrote:

> In 1728 Benjamin Barrett who lived next door built a barn on this site. Before 1830 Deacon [Elisha] Tolman made the barn over or built on its site some shops used by shoemakers and as a printing office. His grandson, Thomas Tolman, converted those into the present house as a dwelling.

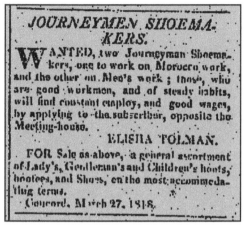

Advertisement in the *Middlesex Gazette*
March 28, 1818
Courtesy Concord Free Public Library Corporation

As you continue toward Monument Square, the cemetery entrance is on your right.

Hill Burying Ground

Concord began burying its dead here as soon as it was settled, but the exact locations of those first graves are unknown. The earliest grave with a legible marker is that of Joseph Meriam, who died in 1677. The most famous grave here is that of John Jack, a man born in Africa, who died in Concord in 1773, having purchased his freedom with money he had earned. His headstone reads,

> Here lies the body of John Jack...
> Tho' born in a land of slavery
> He was born free.
> Tho' he lived in a land of liberty
> He lived a slave.
> Till by his honest, tho' stolen labors,
> He acquired the source of slavery,
> Which gave him his freedom.

This pointed epitaph was written by a Tory attorney, Daniel Bliss, calling out the irony

**Colonel John Buttrick (1731-1797) headstone.
Buttrick's order to fire resulted in the first British
casualties in the American Revolution.**
Hill Burying Ground

of the Patriot cry for freedom. A British officer who dined with Bliss sent home a copy of the text, which was printed in a London newspaper. Bliss fled Massachusetts, as did many other persons loyal to the mother country, and became a judge in New Brunswick.

Leaving the cemetery, turn right toward the square, which was historically part of Concord's Common and its training ground for militia exercises—a boon to the taverns.

Monument Square

St. Bernard's Church

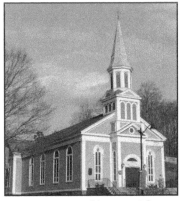

Monument Square

The Green Store, which was kept by a sequence of retailers, occupied this site. This church was erected behind the store, in 1840, by a Universalist congregation, which met there into the 1850s. It was empty until 1863, when it was purchased to become Concord's first Catholic church, which was needed because the numbers of Irish immigrants had increased in the middle of the century. In 1870 the church was lifted, brought forward, turned to face the square, and enlarged. Its present appearance is the result of a renovation in 1889.

Town House

Monument Square

Concord built this brick Town House in 1852, after the town lost the right to hold town meetings in the Middlesex County Courthouse. The architect , Richard Bond, had recently designed the renovations to the First Parish Church. The arched tops of the three second-story windows and other characteristics mark this as an example of the Italianate style of architecture (see page 41). Both the large room used for town meetings and the building itself were referred to, sometimes, as the Town Hall.

This building was Concord's center of social and cultural life. In addition to being used for town administration and police, it had a room for a library, two school rooms, and a dance hall rented out for functions. Concord Lyceum[6] programs were held here. In 1879, when Concord's women won the right to vote in local elections, Louisa May Alcott was the first woman to register, which she did in this building.

Courthouse/Insurance Building

Monument Square

One reason that Concord became a regional commercial center is that it was a shire town—for two centuries county courts met here. These included the Courts of Session, Common Pleas, and the Probate and Supreme Courts. In 1794, Middlesex County built a courthouse here to accommodate this activity.

Court sessions brought many people to town, increasing the need for inns and taverns. Court officials marched diagonally across the square, in their gowns, from the Middlesex Hotel. "September Court Week" was treated as a festival, drawing spectators from surrounding towns, who were entertained by shows and horse races and fed by street vendors on the Common (now Monument Square).

The first courthouse was a center of Concord community activities until it was destroyed by arson in 1849. It was replaced by this building in 1851. In 1867 most county courts were moved to Cambridge and Lowell. County property, including this building, was given to the town, which sold it to the Middlesex Fire Insurance Company.

Cross the street and pass in front of the inn.

Colonial Inn

Monument Square

The northwest end of Monument Square is dominated by the Colonial Inn. From Rev. Peter Bulkeley's estate this land passed to his son-in-law, James Minot, who, before 1716, built the house that remains as the right-hand of the three-part building before you. The middle section was added as a store, which Deacon John White purchased in 1788. He built a house that became the left, or western, end of the building. Deacon White, a pious man not reluctant to correct others, left his pet parrot outdoors in the summer. To the distress of the Deacon but to the amusement of the village, schoolboys taught the parrot to swear.

Daniel Shattuck (1790-1867), who had apprenticed in store-keeping over on the church green, took over the store here on his way to becoming the town's most successful businessman. By 1839 Shattuck owned all three buildings. He was accepted into the Social Circle when he was only twenty-five. In 1861, he gave the buildings to his daughter, Frances Shattuck Surette. She and her husband opened guest quarters at the east end, and named it Thoreau House, after Henry's aunts, who lived there. John Maynard Keyes bought the place about 1890. The inn was subsequently

expanded and has been known as the Colonial Inn since the beginning of the 20th century.

Display advertisement, *Middlesex Gazette*, 1818
Courtesy Concord Free Public Library Corporation

Antique postcard of Colonial Inn
Courtesy Concord Free Public Library Corporation

At the corner, turn right onto Lowell Road and walk a block to Bow Street. Take the crosswalk. The home one of Concord's most vivid characters is just to your left.

Dr. Josiah Bartlett House

35 Lowell Road

This brick house was built by mason Thomas Hunt in 1830. It soon became the office and residence of Dr. Josiah Bartlett (1796-1878). He and his wife Martha Tilden Bradford Bartlett raised a big family here: six sons and three daughters.[7] Dr. Bartlett was a stout abolitionist and was also devoted to the temperance cause.[8] In 1862 he was elected President of the Massachusetts Medical Society. Dr. Bartlett had a reputation for buying fast horses and driving them at top speed, whether he was making a house call or helping people escape slavery by taking them to Fitchburg—one stop nearer freedom in Canada. His minister, Rev. Grindall Reynolds, wrote of him:

> He was outspoken to the last degree, and did not know how to conceal any opinion or feeling, and yet left few or no enemies behind him. He was unlike any other man whom I ever met. His life bore on every part of it the unmistakable impress of his personal peculiarities, his personal feelings and his personal conscience. He carried on his mind and heart the history, the antecedents and the wants of the whole town.

After the last Bartlett daughter died, in 1900, the house was purchased by another doctor with a big family. Theodore Chamberlin and Anne Bixby Chamberlin had eight children, the last of whom lived here until 1970.

Dr. Josiah Bartlett
Courtesy Concord Free Public Library Corporation

Head back to Monument Square. You will pass the Christian Science Church, which was built in 1914. The gable-forward building beyond it has had several uses of historical interest.

Town School/Freemason's Hall

Monument Square

In 1687, Timothy Wheeler donated this land, by bequest, for construction of a schoolhouse. The building we see here was built in 1820 to replace a school that had burned. The Corinthian Lodge of Freemasons offered to help pay for construction of this building if they could have the upstairs for their hall. Henry Thoreau went to grammar school here, and was hired to teach here in 1837, after he graduated from Harvard, but he quit over pressure to use corporal punishment. He and his brother John started a new school in the Old Academy, now on Middle Street.

Concord's social fabric was riven by two great controversies early in the 19th century. The first was religious (see page 36). The second arose when the Masons' secrecy and political influence spawned an Anti-Masonic Party. This antagonism played out across the state and the nation, and was sharply felt here in Concord, where, in the 1830s and '40s, feeling ran high and acrimony was expressed in competing newspapers.

In 1851, when the Town Hall was built, the school (and Lyceum programs) were moved there. The building was privately owned for a time, then, in 1909, it was re-acquired by the Masons.

County House

Monument Square

Continuing toward the Milldam, pass Monument Hall, built in 1907, then rebuilt after a fire in 1947. Next, much closer to the street, is the County House, which has grown from a small wooden house in the early 1700s to the large, brick-clad, mansard-roofed building you see today. It has been the rectory of St. Bernard's Church since 1867. Before that it was owned by Middlesex County. Half of the house was the residence of the jailer and the other half was rented to tenants.

Henry Thoreau famously spent a night in the adjacent jail. The jail is gone, but its location is marked by a plaque. To find it, walk to the back of the grassy lot just past the County House.

Middlesex Hotel Site

The Middlesex Hotel, c. 1870
Courtesy Concord Free Public Library Corporation

At the intersection beyond the rectory is an open space, the site of the Middlesex Hotel, which was built by John Richardson in the late 1700s. On the first floor were barroom, dining rooms, and kitchen. According to Robert Gross,[9] workingmen crowded into the well-heated barroom every morning at 11:00 and again in the late afternoon. Town officials frequented the public room on the second floor. Half of the third floor was a dance hall.

The original hotel burned in 1845 and was rebuilt on the same large scale, but the advent of the railroad and the reduced frequency of court sessions shrank the demand for rooms, and it closed in 1882. The property was acquired by the town, and the building was eventually razed.

Turn right onto the Main Street sidewalk.

The Milldam

As you start down Main Street a lively commercial area stretches before you. The long block of Main Street between Lexington Road and Walden Street is called the Milldam. The area on Lexington Road near the church had once been Concord's center of trade and craft production, but that activity gradually shifted to the Milldam, which grew from the dam that formed the millpond for Concord's first mill—the one Thomas Dane agreed to build for Rev. Bulkeley. The pond has been drained—it had been behind the meetinghouse. Mill Brook now flows beneath the street and the buildings.

In 1826, town leaders organized themselves as the Milldam Company and launched an effort to rid the town center of noisy, smelly enterprises such as smithies and tanneries. The street was upgraded, the mill taken down, and a group of businessmen financed and guided a gradual modernization. The Milldam was called Exchange Street before it became the first block of Main Street.

Milldam, South Side

On the Milldam, it's easier to see the buildings across the street. The first building you see, 3-13 Main Street, was built by James Garty about 1870. It originally had a third story with a meeting hall used by various fraternal and political organizations. The street level shop has housed a meat market, a millinery shop, and a bakery, among other concerns. About 1900, when a streetcar line was built, the waiting room was here.

Milldam

Next door, 15-17 Main Street, is remembered as Urquhart's Bakery. It was built about 1898 by Alexander Urquhart. On the second floor was the tailor shop of Medow and Silverman. By the 1930s, Helen's Restaurant was here. The small adjacent building, #19, was built in 1959. Its architecture is described as "astylistic." It replaced a shoe shop.

Notice the building set back far from the street. Anne McCarthy Forbes[10] contributed information about it to the Massachusetts Cultural Resources Information System.

> This building stands on filled land where the mill pond used to be before the Milldam Company drained it and developed the new commercial area at the foot of Main Street. It was built in the early 1850's as the first fire house at the center, Engine House #1. This fire company was called the Independence Hose Company; hence the name "Independence Court" for this open land behind the Milldam stores.

Having grown up in the neighborhood, Dr. Edward Jarvis (1803-1884) drew this "Profile of the Milldam 1810-1820" from memory. After graduating from Harvard in 1826, Jarvis taught school in Concord and studied medicine under Dr. Josiah Bartlett before attending the Boston Medical School. Dr. Jarvis became a pioneer in the field of public health.

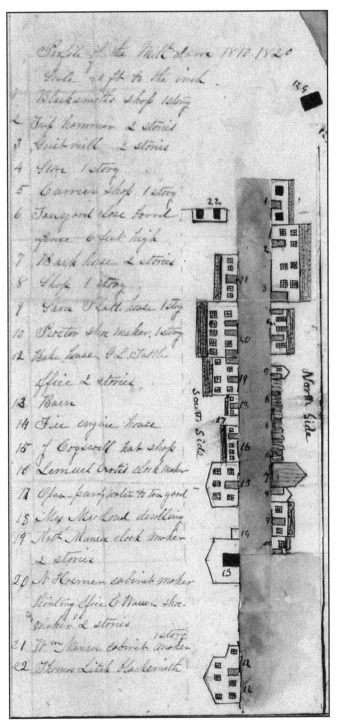

Courtesy Concord Free Public Library Corporation

19

The next two buildings have brick ends that include chimneys.

Milldam

These buildings were constructed soon after the mill pond was drained when the Milldam Company bought these lots, closed the mill, returned mill brook to a free-flowing condition, and began replacing older structures with sturdier, handsomer buildings like these, which were constructed about 1830 either by the Milldam Company itself or by one of its principals, Daniel Shattuck. The buildings have been put to many uses: bookshop, candy store, clothing store, express office, drug store, and jewelry store. Upstairs was a hall used for auctions.

The building that wraps around the corner onto Walden Street was built in 1845. It has housed a general store, a grocery store, a fish market, a drug store, and a shoe store.

Turn your attention to your own side of the street. You are at the Main Streets Market and Café. Just past it, if you would like to see Mill Brook, turn right into the alleyway and walk past the site of the old mill. Mill Brook empties into the Concord River just above the Old Manse and the North Bridge.

Concord Bank

46-48 Main Street

Just past the alleyway is the brick building known historically as the Concord Bank and Middlesex Mutual Fire Insurance Building. Built in 1832, it is the town's first example of the Greek Revival style of architecture. It was built for two new economic ventures, the Concord Bank and the insurance company. Daniel Shattuck was the bank's president. John Cheney was the cashier from its founding until he died in 1869.

A sensational crime was carried out here in 1865. While Cashier Cheney was at his noon meal, the bank was robbed of bonds and cash to the value of $300,000! The perpetrators, Langdon W. Moore and Harry Howard, were eventually caught. The two had thoroughly prepared for the heist, having learned where Cheney hid the key to the safe and having over a series of many nights fitted keys to the building's doors.

On the day of the robbery Moore waited in the South Burying Ground until he saw Cheney lock up and head home for lunch, then he used the fabricated keys to enter the bank and located Cheney's key to open the safe. Howard drove the getaway carriage.

The two were captured because Howard, a professional criminal, was recognized by an old associate, who connected his presence in the area with the fact of the robbery and threw suspicion on the partners. Moore was arrested in New Jersey and much of the loot was recovered.[11]

Newer Banks

The middle bank, 46-48 Main Street, was built in 1894, for both the Concord National Bank and the Middlesex Institution for Savings, which needed more space than they had in the older building.

The last bank you pass is the newest, built in 1932, to house the Middlesex Institution for Savings, which had been incorporated in 1835. Under its revised name, the same bank continues here, fronted by columns deliberately echoing the style of the original bank.

South Burying Ground

Like the Hill Burying Ground, this cemetery was designated when Concord was founded. Ruth Wheeler wrote: "There was a strong English superstition against carrying a corpse across a running stream; indeed, as a practical matter, it would have been hard to carry a bier over the mill brook."[12] The earliest remaining headstone here is in 1697, earlier graves having been marked with wood or not marked. This cemetery was used by the families that settled the southern part of Concord.

Shepherd's Tavern

122 Main Street

The first house on Main Street was Shepherd's Tavern. Before travel by automobile, before street cars, before the railroad, conveyance was by stagecoach. A long-time innkeeper here, William Shepherd, also owned an interest in the stagecoach line that ran west and north to Keene, New Hampshire, a manufacturing center. Stage passengers refreshed themselves here as mail was processed and horses were changed. A later establishment here was called the Coffee House.

The building dates from about 1796. The doorway, with its overhead elliptical fanlight, is considered high-style Federal architecture. Concord Academy,[13] a private secondary school that has come to own many historic houses in this neighborhood, bought this building in 1959.

Coach House

128 Main Street

In the 1830s this building was constructed as an addition to Shepherd's Tavern. The first floor was for coaches; the second floor was a ballroom. About 1856, the railroad having reduced Concord's hotel business, the wing was lopped off and rotated to face the street.

Elnathan Jones/Moses Prichard House

140 Main Street

Elnathan Jones (1737-1793) inherited this lot and surrounding land by from his father, the property having passed through the generations from Elnathan's great-great-grandmother. Elnathan, a successful merchant, built this house about 1780. He had a nearby store that was later moved. The house has characteristics of both Georgian and Federal architectural periods. The Greek Revival porch was added later. The hipped roof is distinctive.

In 1829 Moses and Jane Hallett Prichard bought this house, which remained in the family until Concord Academy bought it in 1947.

One of Moses and Jane's daughters, Elizabeth, departed for a tour of Europe in October 1858, in the company of siblings from next door — Edward and Elizabeth Hoar. Edward and Elizabeth Prichard were married in Florence, in December. They returned to Concord the following September. Their daughter, whom they named Florence, owned this house until her death in 1946.

Elizabeth Prichard Hoar
Courtesy Concord Free Public
Library Corporation

Squire Samuel Hoar House

158 Main Street

Samuel Hoar (1778-1856), known as 'Squire Hoar,' was one of the most powerful and influential men in Concord in the first half of the nineteenth century, and in his later life was considered the leading citizen of the town.

So wrote Anne Forbes of this estimable individual who served in both houses of the Massachusetts legislature and in Congress.

Samuel Hoar
Wiki Commons

He was a founder of the Free-soil Party. In 1844, the Massachusetts Governor appointed him commissioner to South Carolina, where African American seamen were being seized and sold. Hoar traveled south with his daughter Elizabeth to investigate and to challenge the South Carolina law that permitted this. Threatened in Charleston with mob violence, they were secreted from their hotel to a ship and sent home, to the outrage of the Massachusetts public and to the benefit of the anti-slavery cause.

Emerson wrote of Sam Hoar, "The expression of his face is that of a patient judge who has nowise made up his opinion, who fears nothing, and even hopes nothing, but puts nature on its merits. He will hear the case out, and then decide."

Squire Hoar married Sarah Sherman, the daughter of a signer of the Declaration of Independence and the Constitution. She lived in Connecticut; before her marriage Sarah had started a school for Black children in New Haven at a time when it was still illegal there to teach African Americans.

Their eldest daughter was Elizabeth Hoar (1814-1878), who was to have married Ralph Waldo Emerson's brother Charles, but he died during their engagement. She never married, and often stayed with the Emersons, caring for the young and the ill, and helping Waldo with his work. She was a companion to his wife Lidian; together they took the stage from Shepherd's Tavern into Boston to participate in Margaret Fuller's "Conversations."

Something about Elizabeth Hoar's presence left a strong impression. Emerson wrote,

> Elizabeth Hoar consecrates. I have no friend whom I more wish to be immortal than she, an influence I cannot spare, but must always have at hand for recourse. Her holiness is substantive and must be felt,

23

like the heat of a stove, or the gravity of a stone: and Bonaparte would respect her.

He called her Elizabeth the Wise. Emerson's choice of residence in Concord had been due in part to the prospective marriage of Elizabeth to his beloved, gifted brother Charles. The two couples had planned to live together.

Elizabeth Sherman Hoar
Art piece courtesy of the Concord Free Public Library Corporation
Photographic image © 2020 Jim Coutré Photography

The house was begun in 1810 but not completed until Sam Hoar bought and renovated it in 1819. He lived here the rest of his life, and so did Elizabeth after his death. It remained in the Hoar family until 1946. The architecture is a fine example "high-style" Federal.

Bride's House

166 Main Street

This house was at first divided into two apartments. It is called the Bride's House because so many young couples began married life here, including Dr. Josiah Bartlett. Lemuel Shattuck, brother of Daniel and author of Concord's first history, lived here, as for a year did the Thoreau family. This early Federal-style house was built in 1790, as an investment by Josiah Davis, whose home and store were just beyond.

Josiah Davis House

186 Main Street

In 1813, Josiah Davis (1773-1847) built this house and a store next door, which was subsequently moved to Belknap Street. After decades of commercial prosperity, Davis lost his wealth in the financial panic of 1837. His house was purchased by David Loring, a manufacturer of metal products in West Concord, who had a hand in constructing the Fitchburg Railroad[14], the first railroad to serve Concord. Loring bought a house built in the Federal period and altered it, with the addition of columns and porches, to the newer Greek Revival style. In 1888, Samuel Hoar, grandson of Squire Samuel Hoar and son of Judge Ebenezer Rockwood Hoar, bought the place. In 1922 it was the first building of the new Concord Academy.

Ebenezer Rockwood Hoar House

194 Main Street

A bust of E.R. Hoar overlooks the main reading room in the Concord Free Public Library. The sign beneath it reads:

> Like his father Samuel Hoar, Ebenezer Rockwood Hoar (1816-1895) was a lawyer, a key member of the Middlesex Bar, an active citizen of Concord, and a public servant at the state and national levels. A cultivated and sociable man with a good sense of humor, he was as comfortable among members of the Saturday Club in Boston as he was in a court of law. Hoar was one of Ralph Waldo Emerson's good friends.

**Judge E.R. Hoar
by Daniel Chester French**

JOSIAH DAVIS,

INVITES his Customers and the Public to call at his NEW STORE, where he offers for Sale an extensive assortment of Piece Goods, by the latest arrivals, suitable for the season, viz.

	ALL KINDS OF W. I. GOODS.	
Broadcloths,		Silks,
Cassimeres,		Canton Crapes,
Cotton do.		Italian do.
Vestings,		Flag handk'fs,
Calicoes,		Fancy do.
Ginghams,		Ribbons,
Shawls,		Shenille Cords,
Fancy Muslins,		Hosiery
		Linens & Shirtings,
Cambricks,		Cotton Yarns,
Laces for Veils,		&c.

Iron and Steel, Crockery and Hardware, Pork, Bacon, Cheese, &c.

LIKEWISE,
1 Set of Surveying Instruments.
May 11. tf

***Middlesex Gazette*, 1816**
Courtesy Concord Free Public Library Corporation

25

Rockwood Hoar graduated from Harvard College in 1835 and from Harvard Law School in 1839. Politically, he was a Whig, a Free Soiler, and ultimately a Republican. He served as judge of the Court of Common Pleas, a justice of the Supreme Judicial Court, a representative in the United States Congress, and as United States Attorney General in the cabinet of Ulysses S. Grant. A proponent of abolition, he issued a writ of habeas corpus to prevent a federal marshal from taking Frank Sanborn to Washington (see page 34).

Judge Hoar built this Greek Revival house in 1845. When President Grant came to Concord for the centennial of the fight at the bridge, he stayed here, in the home of his former cabinet member. The house remained in the family until purchased by Concord Academy.

President Grant and his cabinet at the E. R. Hoar House
on April 19, 1875
Courtesy Concord Free Public Library Corporation

John Cheney House

204-206 Main Street

This double house was built in the 1820s as an investment by the carriage manufacturer who lived across the street. The bricks for the ends and the chimneys were brought by way of the Middlesex Canal.[15] The two halves of the house were at times under separate ownership. John Milton Cheney lived here for many years, until his death in 1869. Cheney had been the cashier in charge at the bank at the time of the notorious robbery in September 1865.

Continue west on Main Street to the crosswalk at Belknap Street. After you cross, walk a short distance farther west to the yellow house.

Thoreau-Alcott House

255 Main Street

The Thoreau-Alcott House was built by Josiah Davis between 1819 and 1830. John Thoreau, Henry's father, bought it in 1849. He had his pencil-making facility in the barn.[16] Henry kept his boat in the Sudbury River behind the house across the street. He died here in 1862.

Anna Alcott Pratt and Louisa May Alcott bought the house from Sophia Thoreau in 1877, and their parents lived here with Anna and her sons. The wing to the left of the house is said to have been built by Anna as a study for her father, Bronson Alcott.

The Alcotts are associated with three other houses in Concord, as well as the farmhouse at Fruitlands, in Harvard. The Concord houses are the Dovecote (586 Main Street), Orchard House (399 Lexington Road), and The Wayside (455 Lexington Road).

Head back toward the Milldam, to the first house beyond Belknap Street.

William Wilder Wheildon House

207 Main Street

The core of this house is thought to date from the 1700s. It was moved to this location in the 1830s. Sewall Belknap, who helped bring the Fitchburg Railroad to Concord, speculated in real estate in this neighborhood. He lived here before renting and later selling the place to William Wheildon, a journalist, editor, and writer about history and science. Wheildon published a newspaper, the *Charlestown Aurora*.

William Munroe House

185 Main Street

The Munroe house was built in the first decade of the 1800s but received a major make-over around 1845. Its first owner was a baker named Abel Prescott. The Thoreau family lived here from 1827 to 1835. In 1844 the property was purchased by William Munroe, Sr., the cabinet and pencil-maker. Munroe enlarged the house and added Greek Revival characteristics. William and his wife Patty had nine children, several of whom lived here for all or part of the year.

William Munroe Jr. (1806-1877) was born in the County House on Monument Square. He never married. He became wealthy importing textiles and by investing in the mills at Lawrence.

William Munroe, Jr.
Courtesy Concord Free Public Library Corporation

After his retirement from business, Munroe decided that Concord needed a new library. He dedicated himself to planning, financing, managing the construction of, and endowing the Concord Free Public Library. He purchased property, moved buildings, dealt with three levels of government, and reached his goal— the new library was dedicated in 1873.

Cross Academy Lane.

William Whiting House

169 Main Street

In 1820, William Whiting and his wife Hannah Conant Whiting bought a house here that burned in 1823, while Court was in session. Judges, lawyers, jurymen, and ladies all turned out to help pass buckets of water. Probably the brick end walls were in the original structure but were covered with clapboards to hide the effects of the fire. Whiting, introduced on page 10, established his carriage "manufactory" here, in buildings behind the house.

Whiting was a major figure in Concord, a musician (he played the flute), and an activist in the anti-slavery cause. His guests included prominent abolitionists William Lloyd Garrison, Wendell Phillips, and John Brown. His daughters Anna Maria and Louisa Jane were members of the Concord Ladies' Antislavery Society, wrote for anti-slavery publications, and looked after Harriet Tubman when she was in Concord to speak. In the 1860 melee during the attempt to arrest Frank Sanborn (see page 34) Anna climbed onto the marshal's carriage and helped buy time for an angry crowd to gather. Louisa visited South

Yeoman's Gazette
Courtesy Concord Free Public Library Corporation

Carolina long enough to co-author *Influence of Slavery Upon the White Population*, which was notably bold in its treatment of abusive perogatives taken by some male "owners" with enslaved women.

In 1863 this property was purchased by William Munroe, Jr., who removed the carriage shops and re-sold the house.

Return to Academy Lane and turn left toward Sudbury Road. Halfway along, there is an unusual house on your left.

Munroe Gardener's Cottage

29 Academy Lane

A previous structure here was a shop, part of Whiting's carriage-making industry. In 1865, William Munroe Jr. bought this lot, removed the shop, and built this house for the gardener of his family's place across the street.

Later Munroe rented this cottage to E.J. Bartlett and his wife Sally, who was sculptor Daniel Chester French's sister.

This house is considered one of Concord's best illustrations of the Stick Style of architecture that was popular in the period after the Civil War.

Opposite the Gardener's Cottage is Middle Street. Walk down to Number 25.

Old Academy

25 Middle Street

When eight-year-old Willy Whiting started at the Town School on Monument Square, he was subjected to unremitting bullying. His father, William Whiting, learned that the school could not control schoolyard behavior and indeed promoted a culture of violence through corporal punishment. Whiting, an enterprising man, enlisted friends and neighbors, including Squire Sam Hoar and Josiah Davis, and put up this building for a private school. It stood on Academy Lane before it was moved here for the construction of Middle Street.

The original Concord Academy opened in 1823, accepting girls as well as boys as pupils. Henry Thoreau and his brother John attended the Academy, and later taught here. After it closed, in 1837, Henry and John launched their own school in the same building, but that ended with John's tragic death in 1841. William Ellery Channing, companion of Emerson and Thoreau, a poet and biographer, and an admirer of Elizabeth Hoar, lived here for a decade after 1875.

In the early 20th century, painter Charles Hovey Pepper lived here.

Skating **by Charles Hovey Pepper**
Watercolor on paper, 1928
Museum of Fine Arts, Boston
Photograph © 2022 Museum of Fine Arts, Boston.

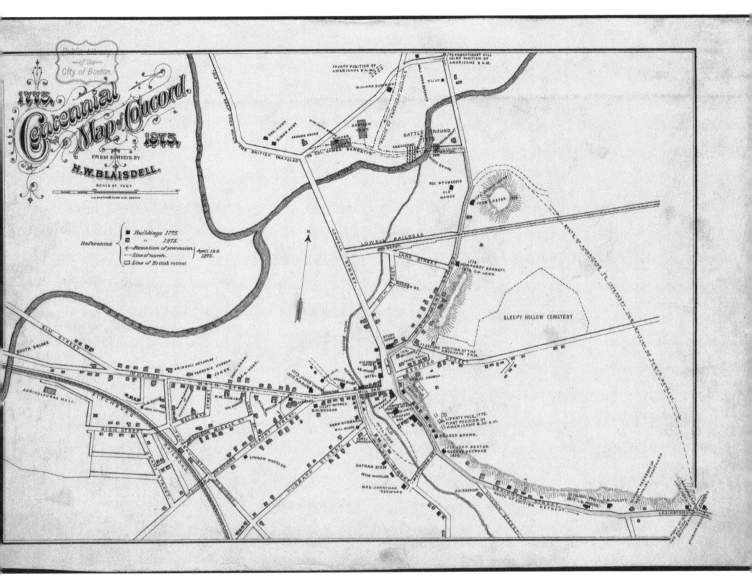

Map for the Centennial of the Battle on April 19, 1775
H. W. Blaisdell
Boston Public Library
Norman B. Leventhal Map Center

31

Return to Academy Lane and turn right toward Sudbury Road. At the corner, turn right again and walk a short distance to 92 Sudbury Road.

Sudbury Road

Edward Bulkeley House

92 Sudbury Road

This house, and its neighbor across the street, are, by American standards, truly old houses. The Edward Bulkeley House is thought to have been built in 1660.

Edward Bulkeley, son of Concord's founding minister Peter Bulkeley, was educated in England. He succeeded his father in the ministry in Concord in 1659. He built this house on Main Street. After his death, in 1694, blacksmith Jonathan Prescott bought it, and it remained in the Prescott family for a century. It was moved to this foundation in 1826 to make room for the construction of Josiah Davis's house and store.

The Norcross sisters, Louisa and Frances, first cousins of poet Emily Dickinson, were later occupants. The sisters, who appreciated

Emily Dickinson sent many of her poems to the Norcross sisters.
Amherst Digital Collections

32

literature, received this poem as a letter from their cousin near the end of her life.[17]

> A tone from the old Bells, perhaps
> Might wake the children.
>
> We send the wave to find the wave,
> An errand so divine.
> The messenger enamored too
> Forgetting to return,
> We make the wise distinction still,
> Soever made in vain.
> The sagest time to dam the sea
> Is when the sea is gone.

Loo and Fannie, as the Norcross sisters were known, lived here until 1908.

Scotchford-Wheeler House

99 Sudbury Road

Like the Bulkeley House, this is one of the oldest buildings in Concord. It is surrounded now by a residential neighborhood, but when it was built it was a farmhouse on agricultural land. John Scotchford, one of the town's original colonists and the first town clerk, was allotted this land before 1653. Probably the

original version of this house was built a few years later. In 1696, the house and barn were sold to Deacon Edward Wheeler and it became the homestead of the large and long-lasting Wheeler farm. Edward's grandson Ephraim was a lieutenant in the Continental Army during the War for Independence. Isabelle Wheeler inherited the farmhouse and owned it until her death in 1955.

Head toward the Milldam—back toward the Academy Lane intersection—and proceed about a block, to 67 Sudbury Road.

Mary Peabody Mann House

67 Sudbury Road

Do you know about the Peabody sisters? Originally from Salem, each of the three had a place among the leading lights of the 19th century in Massachusetts. All three sisters were friends of Elizabeth Hoar. Sophia married Nathaniel Hawthorne, spent her honeymoon at the Old Manse, and lived in The Wayside. Elizabeth and Mary both helped Bronson Alcott at his innovative school, and Elizabeth wrote a book about it that stirred controversy. Mary and Elizabeth were both attracted by the intellect and idealism of education leader

Horace Mann and both waited patiently for a word from him. After years of dithering, Mann proposed to Mary. They married in 1843.

After Mann's death,[18] Mary came here with her two sons, in 1859. Mary lived here until 1866, when she sold the place to Dr. Laura Whiting, a homeopath.

This house continued to be occupied by medical people—in 1889 it was purchased by Dr. George Titcomb, who was a member of Concord's first Board of Health. For Concord's Oral History Program, a patient recalled,

> Dr. Titcomb was one of the greatest doctors we ever had. When you called him, before you had the phone hung up, he would be at the house. In the winter he used to go by horse and sleigh, and when the drifts were so high and the roads weren't plowed and he couldn't get through with the sleigh, he would take the horse out of the sleigh, get on its back and finish his calls.

> Movies used to be held in the Armory on Everett Street and when Dr. Titcomb would go to the movies Saturday night, it would invariably be flashed on the screen that he would have to go back to his office. So he never saw a movie through.

> Dr. Titcomb was great for operating on people particularly taking out their appendix. He was so good at it that he would only take three stitches, he knew just where to cut. And they were afraid to let him go into the library for fear he would take the appendix out of the books.[19]

Frank Sanborn House and Schoolroom

49 Sudbury Road

Franklin B. Sanborn lived in Concord because of R.W. Emerson. At Harvard, young Sanborn was a fan of Emerson's lectures. Emerson recruited him to come to Concord as a teacher. Sanborn's pupils included the children of the period's luminaries: Emerson, Hawthorne, Henry James, Horace Mann, and John Brown.

Frank Sanborn
Wiki Commons

Sanborn was known to have been an ardent supporter of John Brown. After the raid on Harper's Ferry, pro-slavery Senators demanded that Sanborn testify in Washington. He declined. A United States Marshal was dispatched to Concord arrest him. The marshal and his deputies came to this house late in the evening of April 3, 1860. When Sanborn opened the door, the four men overpowered and handcuffed him. Sanborn resisted, bracing his feet on the sides of his door.

Sanborn's sister ran screaming into the street. Among the neighbors who rushed to the scene were Colonel Whiting and his daughter

Sanborn resisting arrest.
Harper's Weekly April 14, 1860
Courtesy Concord Free Public Library Corporation

Anna. By the time the deputies had wrestled Sanborn out of the house, a crowd had gathered, including attorney John Shepard Keyes. Keyes hurried to the Main Street home of Judge Rockwood Hoar to obtain a writ of habeas corpus.

According to Sanborn's account, the sheriff commissioned twenty men out of the mob to act as his posse. After the townspeople had snatched Sanborn away, the marshal and the deputies fled in their now-damaged carriage, hotly pursued by angry Concordians. In the morning Sanford was taken to the courthouse in Boston and released on procedural grounds. Attorney Keyes wrote:

> I came home at night to find Concord stirred to its depths, with reporters and emissaries of all kinds, and more foolish stories in circulation of attacks, and captures, than could be imagined. The papers here and in N.Y. & Washington were filled with it. Congress got excited,

Mason threatened, and it seemed as if war might actually begin. Altogether it was another 19th of April.

No one argues that the Civil War began in Concord—but it was strongly foreshadowed by this incident.

In 1944 the house belonged to Mr. and Mrs. Elmer W. Crouch, who discovered Frank Sanborn's blackboards under three layers of wallpaper in the school room.

Cross to the library.

Concord Free Public Library

Intersection of Sudbury Road and Main Street

The Concord Free Public Library is the result of the initiative and determination of William Munroe, Jr., who persuaded other town leaders such as Rockwood Hoar and Reuben Rice to support the effort. The library was built on the site of the Nathan Brooks house, which had been at one point the Black Horse Tavern.[20]

Designed by Boston architects, the new Victorian Gothic building was an eye-popping addition to what remained quite a small town.

Concord Free Public Library as originally constructed.
McAdow Postcard Collection

The tower was removed in 1917 to make way for the stacks. In the 1933 the building was remodeled, and the style changed to Georgian, under the direction of Concord architect Harry Little. In 2022 the library expanded into an adjacent historic house, that of cabinetmaker William Heywood.

If the library is open, visit the Rotunda, the nave of this temple to books and writers, which is dominated by the Daniel Chester French[21] sculpture of Emerson, who gave the keynote speech at the library's dedication on October 1, 1873.

Leaving the library, cross Sudbury Road and head up the south side of Main Street to the first intersection.

Walden Street

Look down Walden Street to view the Trinitarian Congregational Church. On our 1852 map, the site is labeled "Orthodox Church." This church resulted from a deep division of opinion in the First Parish, which culminated in 1826 when a group left in protest of the liberal theology preached in what became the Unitarian church. Similar fissures took place in many Massachusetts towns around the same time.

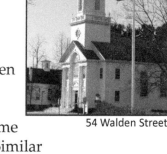

54 Walden Street

This much-admired structure stands on the foundation of the church that burned here in the 1920s. It was designed by Harry Little, who had long studied ecclesiastical architecture in Europe. As you can see, Little took great care with his plan for the steeple.

North Side of the Milldam in the 1890s
Photographed by Alfred Hosmer
Courtesy Concord Free Public Library Corporation

Milldam, North Side

Anderson's Market

42-44 Main Street

Once across Walden Street, you are back on the Milldam. Across Main Street are the buildings you passed earlier in the walk. The first of these, next to the old bank building, known as the Anderson's Market Building, was built by the Milldam Company in 1828. It has been a hatter's shop, Collier's Jewelry Store, and Flint's Grocery. For forty years in the middle of the 19th century, Asa Collier had his clock repair business here. He also sold eyeglasses, jewelry, and other merchandise. Early in the 20th century, the upstairs was the headquarters of the Concord Equal Suffrage League.

Lars Anderson, an immigrant from Norway, bought the building in 1913. He and his family ran a store here for many years. Mill Brook, which runs beneath this building, was used to cool the refrigeration condensers.

Milldam Company Building

36 Main Street

The next building is about the same age as the Anderson Market Building; these two are the oldest buildings remaining on the Milldam. Both were put up by the Milldam Company. Two of Cyrus Pierce's sons, Frank and Arthur, had a shoe store here for fifty years. The building has also housed a gunsmith, a watchmaker, a harness repair shop, and Sing Wah's laundry shop.

This is the same building as above, in 1907.
The dormers were added later.
Courtesy Concord Free Public Library Corporation

Union Block

18-26 Main Street

A large structure called the Union Block stands at the end of the Milldam. It was built in 1881—the mansard roof is an attribute of the Second Empire architectural style. The Union Block replaced three older stores, one of which had burned down along with the stables of the Middlesex Hotel. The building at Number 32 went up in the 1940s to replace one that was torn down.

Albert Vanderhoof bought a hardware and stove business here in 1903; it remains a going concern, much appreciated by loyal customers resistant to "big box" alternatives.

The Union Block has contained a restaurant, grocery store, a meeting hall, a dry-goods store, a tailor shop started by a Jewish immigrant from Lithuania, and Joseph Denaro's fruit dealership—Denaro had immigrated from Italy. Joseph Minute had a combination pool hall and barbershop in this building.

The last stop on our tour is ahead of you on the right, at the corner of Main Street and Lexington Road.

Wright Tavern

1 Main Street

Ephraim Jones (1705-1756) built the tavern in 1747. Four years later he sold it to Thomas Munroe, who had been in the same business down the road where the Adams House was built. The tavern was a popular retreat between church services, during breaks from military training on the square, and for Selectmen's meetings. The militia met here on April 19 when the church bell tolled the warning that the British were on the march, and, when they reached town, British officers refreshed themselves at the Wright Tavern bar.

The Wright Tavern, late 19th century, photographed by Alfred Munroe.
Courtesy Concord Free Public Library Corporation

After the Middlesex Hotel was built on the opposite corner, this building came to be used as a bakery and residence. Francis Jarvis was the baker here in the 1790s, distributing his products over a wagon route, and selling rolls, pies, and doughnuts on training days and when the court was in session. To keep the aging structure from falling apart, town leaders bought it and gave it to the First Parish which has stewarded the historic building and put it to use as an inn, then as a museum and shop, and now as professional offices.

I hope that you have enjoyed learning a little about the buildings along this walk and the lives of people associated with them. Concord is rich in cultural resources, including numerous houses of historic importance not on this tour. West Concord rewards exploration. Iconic destinations, including the North Bridge and Battle Road, the Old Manse, The Wayside, Orchard House, Walden Pond, the Thoreau Birthplace, and Emerson's house, all have their own stories to tell. A few hours at the Concord Museum provides a great introduction.

Antique postcard of Wright Tavern
McAdow postcard collection

Architectural Styles

First Period	Georgian	Federal	Greek Revival
1600-1700	1700 – 1780	1780 – 1825	1825 – 1860
• Steeply pitched roof to shed snow. • Large central chimney for heating the house. • Small windows with diamond-shaped panes. • Often have symmetrical door and window openings.	• Symmetrical; centered front door with windows aligned side-to-side and up-and-down. • Two rooms deep. • Might have gabled, gambrel, or hip roof. • Paneled front doors with a rectangular transom above. • Double-hung windows with small panes.	• Two-story rectangular footprint. • Gable or low-hipped roofs. • Highly decorated front doors, often with semi-circular fanlights for the transom. • Windows in symmetrical rows, usually five per row. • Variable chimney plans include "brick ends" chimneys shown above.	• Gable-forward orientation common. • Entry sometimes on side. • Front door surrounded by narrow sidelights and rectangular transom. • Chimneys less prominent. • Gable or hip roof of moderate pitch. • Porches, either over the entry or the full width of the house, with square or rounded columns.
Colonists adapted ideas brought from England to local conditions and materials. The Munroe/White Cottage is an example of the First Period style (page 4).	Named for the sequence of English kings named George. The Jonthan Prescott House is an example of Georgian style (page 6).	Refinement of the Georgian style. The Samuel Hoar House is an example of Federal style (page 23).	In its era the Greek Revival style dominated public buildings in New England and was used in many residences. Associated American democracy with classical Greece. See the E.R. Hoar House (page 25).

The "saltbox" profile is the result of the original house having been expanded at the rear.

Roof Shapes

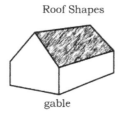

gable

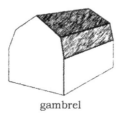

gambrel

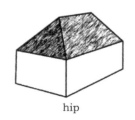

hip

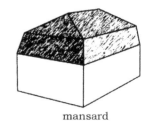

mansard

Gothic Revival	Italianate	Second Empire	Stick Style
1840 – 1880	1840 – 1885	1855 – 1885	1860 – 1890
• Often asymmetrical with L-shaped footprint. • Steeply pitched roofs, often cross-gabled, with overhanging eaves. • Gables commonly decorated. • Windows often extend into gables, frequently with pointed arches. • Tall, thin chimneys.	• Low-pitched roof with widely overhanging eaves. • Tall, narrow windows commonly arched or curved upper sash. • Paired and triple windows frequent; bay windows common. • Often with paired doors and arched doorways surrounded by elaborate decoration.	• Mansard roof, often with dormer windows. • May have roof shingles or slates in colorful patterns. • One or two-story bay windows common. • Tall first-story windows.	• Asymmetrical with emphasis on vertical. • Complex gable roofs, usually steeply pitched with cross gables and overhanging eaves. • Often have decorative trusses on the gables.
These two styles incorporated more relaxed design ideas than their predecessors. Both are associated with the Picturesque aesthetic movement. The Cyrus Pierce House (page 11) is an example of the Gothic Revival style. The Town Hall (page 14) is an example of the Italianate style.		The mansard roof was named for a French architect, Francois Mansart. It was popular during the reign of Napoleon III, France's Second Empire. The County House (page 17) is an example of this style.	The Munroe Gardener's Cottage (page 29) is our tour's example of this lively look.

Stepping back, we note that these styles all rely on square corners and heavy use of wood. Above their granite foundations, external mineral components are limited to glass, some brick, and a few slate roofs. Fire prevention and suppression were greater concerns here than where houses were walled with brick, stone, or adobe. Concord formed a Fire Society in 1794.[22]

The **Queen Anne Style** (1880 – 1910) is represented locally but the structures discussed on our walk are earlier styles.

Architectural style illustrations by Barbara Forman. Roof shapes adapted from Wiki Commons.

Notes

1 Concord's first history was published in 1835. The author was Lemuel Shattuck, brother of the town's leading businessman. Shattuck's book became a model for 19th century histories of Massachusetts towns.

2 Coastal Native American residents had been much reduced by European diseases. The remnant population sometimes regarded English colonists as allies in defense from indigenous groups that remained strong.

3 Some of Concord's hills are bumps in the bedrock, but many, like this one, consist of loose material deposited at the end of the last ice age. These steep-sided ridges were formed by the passage of melt-water streams through canyons of ice. Sand and gravel were deposited by the streams. When the ice canyon was gone, the sand and gravel hill remained.

As the British began their retreat, Patriot forces crossed the North Bridge and skirted behind this high ground to join militia from other towns at Meriam's Corner.

4 *Concord Journal*, 1953.

5 Gambrel refers to that shape we associate with barns: each side of the roof has sections at two different slopes. Having the upper slope shallower increases usable space in the attic—more room for hay in the loft. This particular attic also has dormers to illuminate the interior.

6 The Concord Lyceum adopted its constitution on January 7, 1829. Ezra Ripley was elected President; Deacon Reuben Brown and Josiah Davis were Vice Presidents. Programs in the early decades were lectures and debates. Before the Town Hall was built, the Lyceum met in the old Academy building, the Town School, and at churches. Speakers included Emerson, Thoreau, Wendell Phillips, Oliver Wendell Holmes, James Russell Lowell, Louis Agassiz, Horace Greeley, Theodore Parker, and Jones Very.

7 One of Josiah Bartlett's sons, George Bartlett, wrote a popular guidebook to Concord. It was first published in 1885 and was repeatedly re-issued. George Bartlett promoted canoeing on the Concord River. His guide was a forerunner of this book and of my earlier book about the Concord River. A replica of his boathouse stands on its original foundation behind the Old Manse.

8 Temperance, which meant abstinence from alcohol, or at least from distilled beverages, was a major movement for social change because alcohol was thoroughly woven into New England life. Apples were raised for cider—hard cider was consumed throughout the day. Purchases at stores were rewarded, as lagniappe, with shots of rum. Farm workers expected to be served alcohol at midday by their employers. Then as now, some individuals were incapacitated by addiction, and, then as now, alcohol was tied to domestic violence. Dr. Bartlett's outspoken advocacy of temperance resulted in numerous incidents of vandalism to his property.

9 Robert A. Gross, a historian who researched Concord life-ways throughout his career, published *The Transcendentalists and Their World* in 2021.

10 Anne Forbes gathered and distilled a huge amount of historical information for the Concord Historical Commission. It is now available online at the Massachusetts Cultural Resource Information System. That site will be valuable to those seeking more detailed information about these topics, as will the website of the Concord Free Public Library.

11 Moore was also a career criminal, but until this point he had specialized in counterfeiting. This was his first robbery. He eventually served time in the state prison in Concord and wrote an autobiography: *Landon W. Moore; his own Story of His Eventful Life*, published in 1892. One of his themes in the book is prison reform. Among his suggestions: "It would be well for the governor and council to visit the prison without the usual notice, if they wish to see how the prison is conducted—before and not after the warden has time to prepare to receive company."

12 Wheeler, Ruth R. *Concord: Climate for Freedom*. The Concord Antiquarian Society, Concord, Massachusetts, 1967.

13 Concord Academy, founded in 1922, was established as an upper school for a Montessori school being kept in Josiah Davis's old store. For its first few years it was in the Pellet-Barrett House.

14 Railroads were the transformative new technology of the first half of the 19th century. The Fitchburg Railroad was completed from Boston to Concord in 1844, and through to Fitchburg in 1845. It remains in operation as part of Greater Boston's commuter rail system.

15 The Middlesex Canal, the first major public works project in the new United States, connected Boston Harbor with the Merrimack River at Lowell. Completed in 1803, it crossed the Concord River at North Billerica, where the canal received its water. Although there are shallow bars in the Concord, canal boats were able to bring freight upstream to Concord. The Sudbury River, tributary to the Concord, flows behind the Cheney house; bricks could have been off-loaded there.

16 Ruth Wheeler wrote in 1948:

> Secrecy was traditional in the pencil business from the time in 1812 when William Munroe mixed his graphite, glue, and bayberry wax behind locked doors in his little cottage on Church Green. … Henry [Thoreau]'s discovery of a method of gathering the finest graphite by an air blast and mixing with potter's clay instead of wax, made a much improved pencil. The Thoreaus found that they could sell the finely ground graphite to electrotypers for ten dollars a pound while pencils were six dollars a gross. Henry probably stopped making pencils because the sale of graphite was more profitable. Henry's remark that he had made a perfect pencil so there was no need for him to make any more was typical of him, but it also served to put off questioners who might have discovered this secret source of profit.

17 Emily Dickinson died in 1886. Her last letter was to the Norcross sisters. It read: "Little Cousins, Called Back. Emily."

18 In 1859 Henry Thoreau wrote in his journal:

> Dr. Bartlett handed me a paper today, desiring me to subscribe for a statue to Horace Mann. I declined, and said that I thought a man ought not any more to take up room in the world after he was dead. We shall lose one advantage of a man's dying if we are to have a statue of him forthwith...It is very offensive to my imagination to see the dying stiffen into statues at this rate.

19 Gertrude Hagerty (age 75) and Gladys Cull (age 82) interviewed July 28, 1978, Concord Oral History Program. Renee Garrelick, Interviewer.

20 Residence of Mary Merritt Brooks, the most active member of Concord's Women's Anti-slavery Society, founded in 1835.

21 Sculptor Daniel Chester French (1850-1931) modeled his first major commission, *The Minuteman,* at his studio, which was farther down Sudbury Road than our walk took us. He sculpted *Abraham Lincoln* for the Lincoln Memorial in Washington, D.C. in the last phase of his long career.

22 The town's website states:

> Organized fire protection in Concord dates as far back as 1794 when a Fire Society was formed and owned one small hand engine with a bucket filled tub. Each member of which was required to keep in readiness for use, two leather buckets, a ladder and a large canvas bag. It was expected that each member at the alarm of a fire, would seize his buckets and bag and go to the scene and help save the property from destruction.

The first New England "firemen's muster" was held in 1849. At these events, groups from different towns compete to see which antique "hand tubs" can throw water the greatest distance.

Wiki Commons

Bibliography

Abbott, Mary. Concord Oral History Program Interviewer: Renee Garrelick 1978.

Amherst College Digital Collections. Archives & Special Collections, Emily Dickinson Collection.

Bartlett, George B. *Concord Historic, Literary and Picturesque*, Fifteenth Edition. Boston: Lothrop Publishing Company, 1895.

Boston Public Library Norman B. Leventhal Map Center.

Concord Historical Commission. *Historic Resources Masterplan of Concord, Massachusetts.* Town of Concord 1995, updated 2001.

Concord Free Public Library website and images and information from Special Collections, individually credited above.

Concord Historic Buildings Website of the Concord Free Public Library.

Concord Museum catalogue for 1989 exhibition "Harry Little's Concord: Public and Domestic Architecture, 1914-44," 1989.

Concord, Town of, website, 2022.

Curran, Victor. Personal correspondence, 2022.

Emerson, Edward Waldo and Waldo Emerson Forbes, Editors. *Journals of Ralph Waldo Emerson.* Boston and New York: Houghton Mifflin Company, 1909.

Emily Dickinson Museum website.

Fenn, Mary R. *Old Houses of Concord.* Old Concord Chapter, Daughters of the American Revolution, 1974.

Forbes, Anne McCarthy. *Narrative Histories of Concord and West Concord.* Concord Historical Commission, 1995.

Forbes, Anne McCarthy. Personal correspondence, 2022.

Forman, Barbara, Personal correspondence, 2022.

Forman, Richard, Personal correspondence, 2022.

French, Allen. *Old Concord.* Boston: Little, Brown, and Company, 1915.

Garrelick, Renee. *Concord in the Days of Strawberries and Streetcars.* The Town of Concord, Concord Historical Commission. Concord, Massachusetts: 1985.

Gross, Robert A. *The Minutemen and Their World.* Hill and Wang, New York, 1976.

Gross, Robert A. *The Transcendentalists and Their World.* New York: Farrar, Straus and Giroux, 2021.

Hagerty, Gertrude and Gladys Cull. Concord Oral History Program, Renee Garrelick, Interviewer. 1978.

"Historic New England Architectural Style Guide," Historic New England website.

Jarvis, Edward. *Traditions and Reminiscences of Concord, Massachusetts 1779-1878.* Edited by Sarah Chapin. Amerherst: The University of Massachusetts Press, 1993.

Keyes, J. S., et al. Memoirs of Members of the Social Circle in Concord: 2nd. ser., from 1795 to 1840. Cambridge: Riverside Press, 1888.

The Massachusetts Cultural Resource Information System (MACRIS) https://mhc-macris.net/

Moore, Langdon W. *Landon W. Moore; his own Story of His Eventful Life.* 1892.

Richardson, Laurence Eaton. *Concord Chronicle 1865-1899.* Concord, Massachusetts: 1967.

Robbins, Paula Ivaska. *The Royal Family of Concord; Samuel, Elizabeth, and Rockwood Hoar and Their Friendship with Ralph Waldo Emerson.* 2003.

Smith, Joseph Coburn. *Charles Hovey Pepper.* The Southworth-Anthoensen Press, Portland, Maine, 1945.

Swayne, Josephine Latham, Ed. *The Story of Concord Told by Concord Writers.* Boston: The E.F. Worcester Press, 1906.

Wheeler, Ruth R. *Concord: Climate for Freedom.* The Concord Antiquarian Society, Concord, Massachusetts, 1967.

Wheeler, Ruth R. *Concord Chronicle* and *Concord Journal* history columns.

Index

Details from Middlesex Hotel photograph on page 18
Courtesy Concord Free Public Library Corporation

ISBN: 978-1-7357336-6-1

Library of Congress Control Number: 2022934425

Copyright 2022 Ron McAdow

(No copyright claim on Wiki Commons images.)

Photographs are by the author unless otherwise credited.

The author acknowledges the assistance of numerous individuals and institutions in creating this guide. Anke Voss and Jessie Hopper of the Concord Free Public Library Special Collections provided valuable information and advice. Concord Art, the Concord Museum, the Museum of Fine Arts, and Jim Coutre Photography permitted inclusion of images, and other sources, such as the Boston Public Library, Wiki Commons, and the Amherst Digital Collection made public domain materials available online.

Betsy Stokey, Barbara Forman, Richard Forman, Victor Curran, and Leslie Wilson provided suggestions and corrections that raised the quality—thank you! Larry Buell knew that Emily Dickinson's last letter was to the Norcross sisters, and what it said.

The Rotunda at the
Concord Free Public Library

Ron McAdow's previous non-fiction books are *The Concord, Sudbury, and Assabet Rivers: A Guide to Canoeing, Wildlife, and History*, *The Charles River: Exploring Nature and History on Foot and by Canoe*, *New England Timeline*, *Imaging the Past at Mount Misery*, and, as co-author, *Into the Mountains; the Stories of New England's Most Celebrated Peaks*. His novels are *Ike* and *The Grove of Hollow Trees*. For children, he wrote and illustrated *How Dragons Got Senses* and *The Thunderstorm and Other Songs for Children*.

PHP

Personal History Press
Lincoln, Massachusetts

Printed in the USA
CPSIA information can be obtained
at www.ICGtesting.com
JSHW070453150624
64779JS00008B/61